STRENGTH IN NUMBERS

REGGIE JOHNSON

DEDICATION

This book is dedicated to my nine year old self who picked up this craft not thinking anything would come of it. Then, 9 years later while in college, he picked up the pen once more to discuss the trials, tribulations and situation that occur in everyday life. Now, today, myself and writing are one in the same. I am nothing without it and because of it, the ink never dries up.

PROLOGUE

At first, one may not notice the power a number can withhold. The higher you go, the higher the level of intensity each more stronger than the next. When one can notice the strength in numbers, the possibilities are endless.

Played this game of love for many years so much that this tainted
heart has become blackened charcoal
Engulfed with bursts of flames caused by your mental scars and
bruises
The light you brought in my life did lead unnecessary shadowy
figures that brought darkness
And you did fall in love with them
And you got caught by the element of surprise
Just as I thought you would

Years looking back, it was true
You did not love me like I intended to love you
Plagued my mind for awhile but I moved on
You taught me a lesson
Answered many questions
You sought me out and in the end
You were going to play me from the beginning
I should've just played you first to salvage my own impending
trauma

Who gives a fuck about how long it's been since I've dated someone?
When will I fall in love?
Chasing love in others when I need to love myself first
Not sick of being lonely
Just sick of appreciating myself through others

One admission ticket that we hold onto for our entire life
We take with us when we are awake and when we fall asleep
Just hope that ticket is valid in the afterlife

You had the cheat codes to my heart written down
Memorized
Muscle memory
And you still couldn't get the input I needed from you
Guess we were playing two different systems

I was the king of hearts in your hand
Yet you folded so easily
Too much power for one to possess
And you watched your life points decline
And you wouldn't do anything about it

Times continued to change
Calling you on your cell phone was the 2010s
Now we dive head first into DMs
There's no more initial interpersonal interactions
I can't keep up with the changes

The empire we built
Ended after several seasons
And Lee Daniels couldn't save us from cancellation
We sold some records but
We turned out to be a one hit wonder
And now I can't believe we were ever on the same tune

To the girl that was withering away
I hope you're doing well
I hope you found the light amongst all the dark
You deserve to shine bright in all rooms and not hiding in the
shadows

All I do...
Is think about them lips...
Them hips...
Acrylic fingertips...
As you touched my inner palm
And as I swam through quicksand
I was enveloped by your presence
That I felt like I was in encapsulated
in your hourglass

Let our kisses be the bass
The electricity beyond lips be the high hats
Our body movements create the tempo
Being as smooth and sensual as R&B
Or heavy hitting as hip hop
Our environment creates the soundtrack
to the activity we partake in

Still tired of goodbyes
Not enough of hellos
I think about you day in and day out
Is it hard for you to think of me too?

Focused on my faith
And less about luck
God continues to bless me
Now and more than ever

Late apologies
Led to no one forgiven
You were right
But that didn't make the situation better
You still left

Yes, we live in Sonic's world
Running through life
Chasing after coins
Dealing with our enemies
But what's it like to deal with main character syndrome?
Maybe sometimes I want to be Tails
There's a lot of times my demeanor feels like Knuckles
Life just moves too fast
Trying to keep up can be draining

Love is blind as fuck
My heart beat loudly for months
And then I was able to see
Everything for what it was
Who you really were
Goddamn love should be deaf too

There's nothing more powerful
Than currency
No matter the kind
No matter the type
Anything can be used by money
I've seen it control one's emotions
To the point that it's the most
Destructive entity I've ever dealt with

Actions are better than words
I can leave you speechless
Without speaking less
I can give you every bit of light
Through my camera lens
And it will tell you all how I feel about you

What you got was everything you saw
Everything was crystal clear
Yet you couldn't focus on me
Put away the camera in your phone
And you could've captured memories with me

24

I expected less and I received so much more
Less disappointment that way

We gave up on 21 questions
When you could barely answer the main 5 W's
We ended up this way thanks to you
And no one else

Hello,
It's me...
And not the Adele track
Checking in on you since you left me all those years ago
How did it work out for me?
I'm blessed and that's all you need to know

I still have only said "I love you" to one girl
The next person to come close
Went Casper in 90 days
And who was I gonna call? Ghostbusters?
That wasn't gonna mend this heart

My heart has been on lock for too long
I just want to give my love to someone
Find the key...
It's that easy

Hit after hit
The soundtrack we created
From our emotions
From our thoughts
From our desires
Went platinum in our minds
Sold out many arenas
And we owe it all to you

Right my wrongs
If you can read me my rights
I need to be arrested by your love
If you want me to be invested in you
Right now I can't tell how much you mean to me
No need to write it all down
Just show me

All of me or none of me
Which do you choose?
Are you willing to go the distance?

28 days turned into 28 months later
I'm not counting down any days until I find love
I'm waiting until it finds me

Leap years are special
That extra 1440 minutes
Make me ensure to use it carefully
Meaningfully
Use every extra minute while you have it
Because you may not get to experience it again

It took 30 seconds for you to
Never want to speak to me again
Or so I thought...
You just didn't respect me enough
To explain what was happening
At the time I needed you to
And not your explanation means nothing

The hotline don't bling anymore
It don't ring anymore
And I'm glad it doesn't
But now, we're in the age of notifications
And I hate to see yours pop up

Still wanting to relive the good old days
Growing up was something we wanted a lot
Now that I have I wished I would've enjoyed it more
Time is moving ever so fast

You were literally the Dark Phoenix
Bringing love and rage all in one
Your wings were splattered with the blood
Of everyone who you affected
Including mine

Over the years
I learned that crying is good for healing
Not necessarily have to be pain all the time
And that's fine

Some things are better left of unsaid
But it's most important to get things off your chest
Let out all your thoughts
Don't keep all that energy in
Because when you let it go
Your energy will go with it
Determine how much you want to exude

To the one that got away
Come back...
Just know if I get that chance
I'm not letting go

Don't play with me or be dishonest
But follow the rules of love
Pay attention to each other's love languages
So we can communicate effectively
And not let our true intentions go silent

Being able to distinguish the real from the fake
Has become a skill
It's not a competition
Just a trait that's most important to have

The kink of submission is still present
Can you be dominant?
Can you bring me to my knees?
Can I succumb to your control?

When we were together
Love felt like the NFL Combine
Testing my strength, agility and stamina
And still after everything
You weren't my #1 draft pick

**THANK YOU ALL FOR THE SUPPORT OVER THE YEARS
THIS BOOK STARTED MY WRITING CAREER AND I WANTED TO
REINTRODUCE THIS COLLECTION TO EVERYONE**

-Because the ink never dries up...
-Reggie Johnson

BECAUSE THE INK NEVER DRIES UP

FOLLOW ME ON MY SOCIAL MEDIA

RDJOHNSON.ORG
FACEBOOK: @R.D.JOHNSON
TWITTER: @_RDJOHNSON_
INSTAGRAM: @_RDJOHNSON_